Selected Poems
of
MARY WEBB

Edited with an Introduction
and Notes by
GLADYS MARY COLES

HEADLAND

Selected Poems of
MARY WEBB

*Edited with an Introduction
and Notes by*

GLADYS MARY COLES

HEADLAND

First published 1981
Second Edition 1987

Copyright © Gladys Mary Coles 1981, 1987
this Selection, Introduction and Notes

Published by
HEADLAND PUBLICATIONS
38 York Avenue
West Kirby
Wirral, Merseyside, L48 3JF

ISBN 0 903074 50 8

Acknowledgements to Jonathan Cape Ltd. and
the Executors of the Mary Webb Estate

CONTENTS

PREFACE

In 1981, when *Selected Poems of Mary Webb* was first published, it was my hope that this would bring attention to an aspect of her work hitherto overshadowed by her novels.

Six years later, the demand for Mary Webb's poetry has necessitated a Second Edition of this volume. Its publication both marks the sixtieth anniversary of her death and reflects the continuing growth of interest in her life and work.

G.M.C., 1987

INTRODUCTION

The Shropshire writer Mary Webb (1881-1927), though better-known for her novels, of which the most famous are *Gone to Earth* and *Precious Bane,* was a poet of distinct achievement.

Like Thomas Hardy, whose work she admired, Mary Webb thought of herself as primarily a poet. She was writing poetry before novels; this was her chosen craft, and a compulsion throughout her life. But her poems have received relatively little attention, and it is on her novels — designated by Chesterton as 'the prose poems of a Shropshire Lass'[1] — that her literary reputation, which was posthumous, has rested.

When she died at the age of forty-six, Mary Webb was on the threshold of a break-through to the public success which had evaded her. Her fifth novel, *Precious Bane,* winner of the coveted Prix Femina (for 1924-5), had gone into a fourth printing as well as into the popular Travellers' Library series; she was becoming something of a cult in certain literary and publishing circles, had begun reviewing novels and poetry for the *Bookman,* and was working on her poems in the hope of publication. But she died in comparative obscurity (on 8 October 1927). Six months after her death Stanley Baldwin, in a speech at the Royal Literary Fund Dinner, praised the 'first-class quality' of her writing, and overnight she was discovered by the wider public. To meet the enormous demand for her books, some of which were out of print, Jonathan Cape quickly brought out the Collected Works with Introductions by distinguished writers. This edition included her previously uncollected poems, only a few of which had appeared in print during her lifetime. Containing a group of her nature essays and an Introduction by Walter de la Mare, *Poems and the Spring of Joy* was published in 1928 and reprinted many times in the Thirties. That hurriedly assembled collection was thought to be all that existed of her poetry.

There were, however, other poems as well as fragments among her manuscripts, found later by her husband and literary executor Henry B. L. Webb. He included ten of these in *A Mary Webb Anthology,* compiled shortly before he died in 1939; and he prepared a second collection, which was ready for publication at his death. *Fifty-One Poems* was eventually brought out after the Second World War, with wood engravings by Joan Hassall.

During research for my biography of Mary Webb, *The Flower of Light* (1978), I tracked down a further group of unpublished poems, and also drafts and alternative versions of poems in the two posthumous collections. These manuscripts (autograph and typewritten) had been sold by Henry B. L. Webb during the Thirties. I included a number of these pieces in my edition of her hitherto ungathered and unpublished writings, *Mary Webb: Collected Prose and Poems* (1977).

It seemed to me then that a new selection of her poetry was needed, drawn from the three groups published over a space of fifty years. While engaged on the biography I began to prepare this selection. Since then there has been a great revival of interest in her work, but the two earlier collections are now out of print. Clearly the publication of this volume is timely and, in 1981, appropriate, as it marks the centenary of her birth.

*

While Mary Webb as a poet does not belong to that 'higher cleave' (in Gerard Manley Hopkins' phrase), her work nevertheless merits wider recognition than it has been accorded. Several points deserve attention.

First, Mary Webb is a fine 'country' or nature poet. In this tradition of English poetry, she stands with John Clare for her precise observation, her naturalist's knowledge and the joy in nature with which her words are charged (especially in the earlier poems). As a reviewer of natural histories for the *Spectator* during the Twenties, she looked, above all, for accuracy in the books under review: her own accuracy is seen in her sensory descriptions, and in the clarity and particularity of her imagery. Years of immersion in nature, of first-hand knowledge, inform her poetry; telling detail invests with authenticity such nature poems as 'Foxgloves', 'The Snowdrop', 'Little Things', 'The Water Ousel' (reminiscent of Clare's bird poems). As Wilfrid Gibson said, in a review of *Poems and the Spring of Joy*: 'Mary Webb's gift was something more exquisite, more searching than acute observation; it was an intuitive and tender intimacy shared with birds and beasts and flowers.'[2]

She knew indeed 'the perfume thrushes smell' ('In April'), 'the peculiar scent of every tree' ('Farewell to Beauty'), 'the rope-walk of the honeysuckle' ('The Wood'), 'the ancient roads/In the leaf of a nettle' ('The Secret Joy'). Her senses were of 'microscopic keenness' (Martin Armstrong),[3] 'rarely delicate' (de la Mare)[4], and served her well in the choice of sharp simile and metaphor. Her bond with nature was one of the mainsprings of her writing, and indeed a lifeforce. The intimacy and intensity of this relationship is evident throughout both poetry and prose, from the earliest extant work to the last. In this sense, all her nature poems are personal.

Mary Webb's youthful work is largely descriptive, drawn from impressions of the countryside and the changing seasons. As it develops, the expressions of her response to the natural world are increasingly reflective, though without any loss of the sense of wonder. In 'Sallow Catkins', for instance, her close observation moves out to a cosmic view and, in the final stanza, she relates each of these perceptions to human life and destiny, drawing inferences. In her later work, aspects of nature become representative of her states of mind and feeling. Always her imagery is drawn from nature, but the movement is from the outer landscape to the inner. Of course, for her, nature meant specifically — and supremely — the Shropshire countryside of the Welsh Border: this was the source of her inspiration, the setting of her work, the landscape which from early childhood had worked on her imagination and quickened her sensibilities.

Sometimes in her nature poems she expresses, like Wordsworth, a sense of the immanence of a creative spirit or presence. Poems such as 'The Vagrant', 'Presences', 'The Spirit of Earth' are imbued with mystical intuition, with apprehension of the infinite in the finite. And at her best she can convey, as did Gerard Manley Hopkins, a perception of the individuality and the unity of all things in creation.

Nor has Mary Webb been sufficiently recognised as a woman poet. In the context of her time this is particularly regrettable, for there had been hardly any women poets of distinction before (Elizabeth Barrett Browning, Emily Brontë, Christina Rossetti, Emily Dickinson, Alice Meynell, Charlotte Mew). A few critics made claims for her after the publication of *Poems and the Spring of Joy.* T. Earle Welby, for instance, rated her highly. He praised her quintessential quality of 'gravity in joy' and noted the parallel with John Clare.[5]. In *The Time of Yeats* (1937), Cornelius Weygandt observed 'the littleness of accomplishment, in the aggregate, of women in verse as compared to the largeness of their accomplishment in prose' and pointed to Mary Webb's achievement in both fields.[6]. Her poetry is certainly not a by-product of her novels: always a poet, she was writing from the age of six and during a long apprenticeship was concerned with technique, attentive to metre and rhyme, practising sonnets, rondeaus and other forms. It is worth noting, too, that Mary Webb, in reviews and articles, made some interesting statements revealing her understanding of her art. For instance, reviewing the poetry of Morton Luce (1925) she commented that overemphasis on 'perfection of form' sometimes results in 'loss of spontaneity and accuracy of idea'.[7] In a remarkable article, 'The Core of Poetry' (*The English Review,* 1920), she put forward her views on what poetry is, its source and significance, emphasising the importance of the unconscious in the creative process. From her own creative experience she was aware of that quickening in 'the poet's deepest self': from here true poetry emanates and in this 'the subconscious, with low, inward-sounding whisper arrests us.'[8]

Thirdly, as a Shropshire poet so evocative of her region, Mary Webb has been undervalued, overshadowed by A. E. Housman. Although it is Housman's name which is generally associated with the county because of his highly successful *A Shropshire Lad,* it is Mary Webb who is more completely the Shropshire poet. While *A Shropshire Lad,* first published in 1896, chimed with the mood and sentiments prevalent during the Great War (thereby becoming immensely popular after 1914), there is little of the real Shropshire in these poems. To Housman, a Worcestershire man, born and brought up near Bromsgrove from where some of the Shropshire hills can be seen on a clear day, the county in his resonant, ballad-like poems is a landscape remote and vague, distantly gleaming, symbolising his boyhood 'land of lost content'. In *A Shropshire Lad,* Housman's poetry has other merits, other concerns, but the authentic particulars of Shropshire are few and sometimes inaccurate (Hughley, for example, does not have a steeple); and it is mainly the frequent use of place-names which creates the sense of place.

The poetry of Mary Webb is rooted firmly in the hills, woods and fields of her native region: the word Shropshire never occurs and actual names are mentioned only twice (Viroconium, Shrewsbury), yet a powerful sense of place is evoked. Her poems are imbued with her feeling for and knowledge of the south-west Shropshire countryside which was her world: its impact upon her was sensuous, spiritual, lifelong. Again and again, in poems such as 'The Plain in Autumn', 'On the Wild Hill', 'Dust', 'My Own Town', 'The Little Hill', 'Absence', while the external scene is described with characteristic lucidity and detail, at the same time the essential atmosphere of the landscape is conveyed. Mary Webb absorbed totally the spirit and moods of Shropshire and these became her own, permeating her words.

One of the essentials of an artist is, as Walter Bagehot put it, an 'experiencing nature': this, certainly, Mary Webb possessed. She is primarily a lyric poet, her work expressive of experience and feelings rather than thoughts. In her poetry she does not intellectualise or moralise and is not didactic (as she sometimes is in her prose); she had an intensely romantic temperament and her poems are deeply-felt personal songs, the dominant themes traditional ones of love, transience, death. The human interest is strong: sorrows, fears, longings haunt her lines; her joy is 'as keen as pain' and often fuses with suffering; love poems reveal her Messianic passion for Henry B. L. Webb, the occasional character pieces her tenderness for others (Douglas, her brother, in 'To G.D.M., or a dead old woman, or Anne Everard, immortalised in 'Anne's Book' like Hardy's 'Lizbie Browne'); her own childless state is poignantly recorded in 'The Neighbour's Children'. Humour, a gentle irony, are not absent. But more often a sense of loss pervades her words, as in the moving, elegiac poems to her father or those arising from anguish at the deterioration of her marriage, or again, those written out of acute hiraeth for Shropshire. The emotional charge in these poems is all the more effective for her artistic control, the result of years of commitment to craft.

In contrast to Mary Webb's many poems of affirmation and celebration are those in which she expresses a dark, tragic view of human existence resembling that of Hardy or Housman. There were times when doubt and depression assailed her, particularly during the First World War, or in the spiritual wilderness she experienced following the death of her father. In this loss of belief, when she abandoned 'the fugitive and fond/Dream of a following music' ('Today'), she communicates her tragic vision; compassion for humanity is the impulse behind poems such as

'The Door', 'Dust', 'The Watcher'. There is a sad resignation in her attitude, reflecting on mortality, the press of time, the ultimate unknown, implicit in the imagery of 'Sunset', explicit in the arresting sonnet 'Swallows':

> Flight is our life. We build our crumbling nest
> Beneath the dark eaves of the infinite,
> We sing our song in beauty's fading tree,
> And flash forth, migrant, into mystery.

Though a minor poet, with no great range of reflection and a general simplicity of style and subject-matter, Mary Webb, nevertheless, has the gift of conveying her vision with freshness, sharpness, directness. She is not linguistically adventurous, not an innovator, is conventional in rhyme and metre, yet she has her own distinctive voice and her poetry is invested with singular charm and sincerity. At times, in expressing her awareness of the physical world she achieves a Keatsian sensuousness and richness — as this, for example, in 'The Plain in Autumn': 'Memoried deep in Hybla, the wild bee/Sings in the purple-fruited damson tree'; or this: 'lissom, rosy pines with wild black hair' ('Humble Folk').

Mary Webb is typically Celtic in her lyricism, her oneness with nature and responsiveness to its mystery as much as to its beauty. The Celtic element in her parentage was strong — her mother, Sarah Alice Scott, was the only daughter of a wealthy Edinburgh surgeon (reputedly connected by clan with Sir Walter Scott); her father, George Edward Meredith, was a Salopian proud of his Welsh descent (by tradition a line from Prince Llywelyn). It was probably Mary's great-grandfather, John Meredith, who had migrated across the Border, settling in Church Stretton: thereafter the Merediths kept up their connections with their Welsh cousins, the Warrens, who owned an estate in Cardiganshire on the slopes of Plynlimon. Mary Webb liked to speak of her Welsh blood and, in conversations with friends, often referred to bardic poetry and to what she called 'the Mabinogion of my ancestral country'.

As a child Mary Webb had been steeped by her father not only in a love of nature and its minutiae, but in the folklore of Shropshire and the Welsh Border. George Edward Meredith, an Oxford M.A. in Classics, tutor and country gentleman, was himself a fairly prolific poet, inheriting the gift from his mother and grandmother — verse was frequently his method of communicating with his wife and children (Mary was the eldest, by six years of six children). He knew a great number of ballads and folksongs and had a repertoire of his humorous verses which he used to sing 'at entertainments for charitable purposes'. In this Mary Webb was like John Clare and Thomas Hardy whose fathers brought them at an early age into contact with folksongs and traditional oral culture. Her father also steeped her in the riches of the English language, educating her at home, where he ran a boarding school in their large country house. Later, her governesses took over, one of whom, Miss Lory, concentrated on the study of Shakespeare and major poets of the nineteenth century; then a two year period away at a Finishing School completed Mary's formal education. Not satisfied, and too delicate in health to pursue the idea of a university degree, she took a Cambridge University Extension Course in English Literature, reading intensively in poetry and the novel. Soon after this she met and married a Cambridge graduate, Henry B. L. Webb, attracted partly by his mind, his literary ability and the fact that he was, like her father and grandfather,[9] a classical scholar, a schoolmaster and, not least, a lover of nature. Initially their relationship had much in common with that of the Brownings: there was ardour and mental stimulation as they exchanged poems and essays (Henry wrote a verse epic on Gilgamesh). Ultimately though, Mary was to learn through bitter personal experience the truth of Ernest Renan's statement about the Celts mistaking dreams for realities, this evident in her last poems.

*

I had two principal aims in preparing the present selection: I intended it to be more representative of Mary Webb's poetry as a whole than any yet in print, thereby doing justice to her achievement; and I hoped to show, by my arrangement of the poems, her development from the earlier work of her twenties to the mature work of her forties. I decided on presentation in sections based on chronological order, grouping together poems written at approximately the same period (dates ascertained from my close study of manuscripts in private collections and from Henry B. L. Webb's dating in some instances). It was not possible to place the poems in strict sequence of composition as this cannot be definitely established, but the loose chronological groupings have several advantages: they bring out the relationship between poems written at roughly the same phase in her life; they show the development in her technique and imagery; and, read in this order, the poems make up a partial, fragmented biography of her emotional and inner life, revealing some of the influences — environmental, personal, external — which shaped her as a person and an artist.

The earliest work, her extant juvenilia, is not included here — examples of this can be found in *Mary Webb: Collected Prose and Poems*. The work in *Selected Poems* belongs to the three decades of her adult life: I have divided it into two sections, Earlier Poems and Later Poems, the demarcation date being 1916, the year of her emergence as a published novelist and a watershed in her literary career and personal life.

While I have not the space here to give my reasons for inclusion or exclusion of poems, I should perhaps explain the sections and their subdivisions.

Earlier Poems covers the years from 1902 to 1916, a period beginning with her struggle back to health after being afflicted with Graves' Disease then incurable) — nature was her solace, refuge and church, her source of renewal and creative impulse. The first set in this section mirrors her keen involvement: these poems celebrating nature are typical of many she was writing in her twenties, a great number of which she destroyed in dissatisfaction as she was consciously striving to develop her technical skill and shed her influences. The subdivisions which follow are my arrangement into series of related poems. A sad series flowed out of deep grief on her father's death (5 January 1909); a series of early love poems to Henry B. L. Webb was written during the first years of their relationship, before their wedding (1912) and after, when they were living at Weston-super-Mare (where Webb was teaching) and then back in Shropshire, at Pontesbury. It is interesting to see how the change to a coastal environment influenced her imagery in the Weston-super-Mare poems 'Isolde' and 'Today', whereas the imagery of 'Humble Folk' is drawn from her immediate surroundings at Rose Cottage, Pontesbury. Poems in the Pontesbury series belong to the period after her ecstatic return to Shropshire (1914) and before the tragedy of the Great War intensified — a happy, fulfilled phase for her, living near the inspiring hill country, writing her first novel, and selling the produce of their garden in Shrewsbury Market as part of her war effort (hence 'Market Day'). A group of poems written during the First World War reflects the effect of the war on the English countryside (as seen by a countrywoman), its influence on her mind and spirit, particularly after the carnage of the Somme, her depression when living at Chester ('An Estray', 1916), and her constant worry about her three brothers at the Western Front.

Under Later Poems I have assembled work from approximately late 1916 to her death in 1927. This section includes poems from her prolific period at Lyth Hill when she made considerable progress in her literary career, and from the increasingly unhappy London phase (1921 onwards). The later poems to, or concerning, Henry B. L. Webb reveal Mary's intense love for him, the sad consequences, her 'agony of loss' (allegorised in the tormented, haunting 'Colomen'). Among her finest work are the last poems which have a yearning undertone, an emotional immediacy arising from her intimations of death. The prevailing mood of these final poems is one of farewell — a sense, keenly felt, of imminent separation from the beauty of the physical world and from nature, ongoing, indifferent. Memorable pieces such as 'Goodbye to Morning', 'To a Blackbird Singing in London', 'The Birds Will Sing', 'Farewell to Beauty', were written when she was slowly dying from Graves' Disease and pernicious anaemia.

Speaking of Mary Webb's art and its grounding in personal experience, Walter de la Mare noted: 'few writers indeed have left behind them so rich a posthumous gift'. During her lifetime, de la Mare was among the first to recognise Mary Webb's talent, to encourage her, inviting her to his Sunday gatherings at Anerley, and to anthologise her poems, selecting three ('Green Rain', 'The Water Ousel' and 'Market Day') for inclusion in *Come Hither* (1923), a volume for 'the young of all ages'. Knowing

Mary Webb's concern with form, de la Mare discerningly commented of her work that 'even though an apparent spontaneity may be only apparent, this poetry is at its best when it *seems* most spontaneous.' Fittingly, it was de la Mare who later wrote the Introduction to *Poems and the Spring of Joy.* The editor of the *Bookman,* A. St. John Adcock, also thought highly of her poetry as well as of her critical ability, engaging her to review for the journal and anthologising two poems ('An Old Woman' and 'Foxgloves') in the *Bookman Treasury of Living Poets.* But apart from this — and the occasional publication of poems in the *English Review,* the *Spectator* and elsewhere — she did not gain that much-desired recognition as a poet before her untimely death.

Mary Webb is like her contemporary Edward Thomas in that they both wrote with quiet sincerity of the English countryside from the 'inside' viewpoint of genuine countrypeople; both were published posthumously and, while they had not appeared in any of the Georgian Anthologies, they were unfortunate in being regarded (or disregarded) as Georgians at a time when this 'school' had fallen into opprobrium (a reaction continuing during the politically and socially conscious Thirties when country poems were out of fashion). As with the poetry of Edward Thomas, there is in the work of Mary Webb a surface similarity in subject-matter to the Georgians — but her voice is individual and her poems, as de la Mare said, 'are more than usually her very self's'; furthermore, as Wilfrid Gibson pointed out: 'though Mary Webb is essentially what is called a nature poet, she has little in common with the Weekend School of poetical reporters, very few of whom have her truly profound knowledge of the life of birds and plants.' Her poems from first to last are indeed 'of the lovely earth' (de la Mare) and her work has an inherent unity. While not quantitatively small (more than two hundred poems are extant), it is finer in quality than that of some better-known Georgians, in spite of the occasional metrical lapse and inexpert rhyme, repetition of her effects and, here and there, a touch of faery. But she left behind a sufficient number of strong, finely achieved poems to indicate that she may well have developed in her maturity beyond certain thematic, linguistic and structural limitations. Lastly, in assessing Mary Webb as a poet, it should be kept in mind that her poems as we have them may not have been her finally revised versions had she lived to complete the preparation for publication.

Gladys Mary Coles

. G. K. Chesterton, Introduction to *The Golden Arrow* by Mary Webb (Cape, Collected Edition, 1928)
. Wilfrid Gibson, 'The Poems of Mary Webb', *The Bookman,* February 1929, pp. 269-70
. Martin Armstrong, Introduction to *Armour Wherein He Trusted* by Mary Webb (Cape, Collected Edition, 1929)
. Walter de la Mare, Introduction to *Poems and the Spring of Joy* (Cape, Collected Edition, 1928)

5. T. Earle Welby, 'Mr. Pound and Others', *The Saturday Review*, CXLVI (22 December 1928) pp. 851-52
6. Cornelius Weygandt, *The Time of Yeats*, (London & New York, 1937) pp. 414-18
7. Mary Webb, 'Morton Luce', *The Bookman*, June 1925, pp. 148-50; reprinted in *Mary Webb: Collected Prose and Poems*, edited with an Introduction by Gladys Mary Coles (Wildings, Shrewsbury, 1977)
8. This article is reprinted in *Mary Webb: Collected Prose and Poems*
9. Reverend Edward Meredith (1793-1873), educated at Oxford, Headmaster of Newport Grammar School; George Edward Meredith was educated at Newport Grammar before St. John's, Oxford.

EARLIER   POEMS

SALLOW-CATKINS

Above a small blue sky of pond
The sallow waves her catkins to and fro.
Round every golden ball there swings
A host of little flies with flaming wings -
Like planets round their travelling sun they go,
With all the limitless blue air beyond.

Above our sedgy destinies
The suns go down their circling, unknown way;
Like catkins on the osier tree,
Each with its worlds of fleet ephemerae,
In close-curbed liberty they sway
On the profound and limpid silences.

So - like the flies that burn and swing,
The suns, that fade like blossom on a tree;
Too small to offer praise, too great
For fear of the Unknown - let us create
The one thing we were meant to be,
And make our own appointed journeying.

TO LIFE

Fair, fierce Life! What will you do with me?
        What will you make me?
        Take me and break me,
        Hurt me, or love me,
But throne me not lonely and safely above thee,
        Sweet Life!

Radiant, terrible Life! See now, I offer thee
        Body and spirit.
        Let me inherit
        Agony - wonder:
But leave me not icily, numbly asunder,
        Dear Life!

THE HERITAGE

Dull?...When the full moon slips in silver past my window-pane,
Just as she slipped by the porphyry arch and shone on Sappho dreaming;
And winds that howled round Nineveh's walls and brought old Babylon rain
Come, like ravens with wide black wings, to waken me with their screaming

Sad?...When my saffron crocus holds a brown bee in its cup,
Just as on Hybla's purple hill, where the honey was warm and yellow;
And every day in my quiet room the crystal light stands up
Pure and sweet as on Olivet when the autumn days grew mellow?

THE LOST ORCHARD

Never in those lonely meadows lingering,
Shall I see the twilight any more;
Never hear the golden water fingering
Pale tansy shadows from the shore;

Never, when the dark thorn hedge is quickening,
Watch the white narcissi upward steal:
Nor, in the pink orchard's hazy thickening,
Hear the early bird-song thrill and peal.

Yet within my heart, where none can ever see,
Blows the apple tree and flows the stream:
Through the violet fields I move, as shadowy
As a fish within the water's gleam.

BOUNTY

The full woods overflow
　Among the meadow's gold!
A blue-bell wave has rolled,
　Where crowded cowslips grow.
The drifting hawthorn snow
　Brims over hill and wold.
The full woods overflow
　Among the meadow's gold;
The ditches are aglow!
　The marshes cannot hold
Their kingcups manifold.
　Heav'n's beauty crowds below,
The full woods overflow!

THE WATER OUSEL

Where on the wrinkled stream the willows lean,
And fling a very ecstasy of green
Down the dim crystal, and the chestnut tree
Admires her large-leaved shadow, swift and free
A water ousel came, with such a flight
As archangels might envy. Soft and bright,
Upon a water-kissing bough she lit
And washed and preened her silver breast, though it
Was dazzling fair before. Then twittering
She sang, and made obeisance to the Spring.
And in the wavering amber at her feet
Her silent shadow, with obedience meet,
Made her quick, imitative curtsies too.
Maybe she dreamed a nest, so safe, so dear,
Where the keen spray leaps whitely to the weir;
And smooth, warm eggs that hold a mystery;
And stirrings of life, and twitterings that she
Is passionately glad of; and a breast
As silver white as hers, which without rest
Or languor, borne by spread wings swift and strong,
Shall fly upon her service all day long.
She hears a presage in the ancient thunder
Of the silken fall, and her small soul in wonder
Makes preparation as she deems most right,
Re-purifying what before was white
Against the day when, like a beautiful dream,
Two little ousels shall fly with her down-stream,
And even the poor, dumb shadow-bird shall flit
With two small shadows following after it.

FOXGLOVES

The foxglove bells, with lolling tongue,
Will not reveal what peals were rung
In Faery, in Faery,
A thousand ages gone.
All the golden clappers hang
As if but now the changes rang;
Only from the mottled throat
Never any echoes float.
Quite forgotten, in the wood,
Pale, crowded steeples rise;
All the time that they have stood
None has heard their melodies.
Deep, deep in wizardry
All the foxglove belfries stand.
Should they startle over the land,
None would know what bells they be.
Never any wind can ring them,
Nor the great black bees that swing them –
Every crimson bell, down-slanted,
Is so utterly enchanted.

A RAINY DAY

With weights of tears the bluebell broke,
The tall white campion wept in sleeping,
And all the humming honey-folk
A fast were keeping.

The fairy people flouted me,
Mocked me, shouted me –
They chased me down the dreamy hill and beat me with a wand:
Within the wood they found me,
Put spells on me and bound me,
And left me at the edge of day in John the Miller's pond.

Beneath the eerie starlight
Their hair shone curd-white;
Their bodies were all twisted like a lichened apple-tree;
Feather-light and swift they moved,
And never one the other loved,
For all were full of ancient dreams and dark designs on me.

With noise of leafy singing
And white wands swinging,
They marched away amid the grass that swayed to let them through:
Between the yellow tansies
Their eyes, like purple pansies,
Peered back on me before they passed all trackless in the dew.

LITTLE THINGS

Among the purple buds, like laden censers,
Careless upon the wind the catkins swing;
They lay a golden spell upon the morning.
From their soft glee how many trees will spring?

The tiny spiders on wych elms in May,
Of rare pale green; the young and downy bee,
Singing her first low song; the white ant's cradle -
They crowd upon us with their mystery.

The fourfold creamy blackthorn buds are folded
Close on green marvels, as upon a treasure
A child's hand; the five pearl doors open softly -
There's a gold house where some elf takes his pleasure.

On the small pear-bud, with its silver calyx,
Some one (I know not who) has set a cross,
Rosy and glowing. On that Calvary-rood
Love might hang long, and know not pain or loss.

Fire-white from curtains of intensest blue
The centre of the speedwell gleams; so fair,
So mystic-frail the tremulous pollen-worlds,
Divinity itself seems slumbering there.

THE SNOWDROP

Three softly curved white sepals veined with light,
Three green-lined petals, guarding frugal gold,
And all so strong to fold or to unfold!
Snow thunders from the bending pines. How slight
This frail, sheathed stem! Yet all unbent it springs,
So swift in stoopings and recoverings.

In the pale sunshine, with frail wings unfurled,
Comes to the bending snowdrop the first bee.
She gives her winter honey prudently;
And faint with travel in a bitter world,
The bee makes music, tentative and low,
And spring awakes and laughs across the snow.

CATERINA TO CAMOENS

O Luiz, Luiz! In those early days
You little thought what bitter tears would flow
When you knelt down and laid your first fresh bays
Before my feet, and kneeling watched me go.
And when you crowned me with your noble praise,
And breathed - 'My Lady!' - reverently and low,
You never dreamed how lonely were my ways
For your - 'My Love!' - which I might never know,
Because the dust - such golden dust to me -
Was thick about you, in a place apart
With weary rest you circled in my heart,
And haloed me with immortality.
But (Mother of grief and love, forgive me this!)
I would have given all for Camoens' kiss.

HAZEL BUDS

Now breaks the sheath and spreads the leaf!
The bank beneath, the branch above,
Are set with nests, are homes of love.
So goodbye,grief!

With restful haste and gentle strife
Pink hazel stipules are unfurled,
Pink dawns are flung across the world.
So welcome, life!

ON THE HILLS

Buffet on sweet buffet, the wildwood came,
Like a green wave or a green flame,
With melodies
And delicate fragrances
And the secret souls of the watching trees.

Colour on grave colour sleeps the ancient moor,
With its blue roof and its purple floor -
Where small birds fly
With merry, pencilled eye,
And like great gods the stately clouds go by.

There's nothing still in the busy world.
Breezes ruffle the wings that are furled,
Seeds go dancing across the meadow,
The pine-tree plays with her dancing shadow,
And ever, beneath the rough elm bark,
The river of sap flows on in the dark.
Far in the mountain, under the sea,
Invisible atoms mysteriously
Move to the making of valley and dune,
Marching on to an unheard tune.
Like homing birds the red clouds fly
At dawn. Like water the stars flow by.
Delicate flowers, each on her stem,
Dance with the leaves surrounding them,
And every weed and shell of the ocean
Answers the tide with a rhythmic motion.

THE SHELL

What has the sea swept up?
A Viking oar, long mouldered in the peace
Of grey oblivion? Some dim-burning bowl
Of unmixed gold, from far-off island feasts?
Ropes of old pearls? Masses of ambergris?
Something of elfdom from the ghastly isles
Where white-hot rocks pierce through the flying
                                        spindrift?
Or a pale sea-queen, close wound in a net of spells?

Nothing of these. Nothing of antique splendours
That have a weariness about their names:
But - fresh and new, in frail transparency,
Pink as a baby's nail, silky and veined
As a flower petal - this casket of the sea,
One shell.

THE VAGRANT

Who came so close then? –
Brushed the wet lilac into mellow laughter;
Set the smooth blackbird at his golden weaving
Making no stir at all, no footprint leaving;
Travelling westward, all things following after?

Who whispered secrets? –
Tempted the worm up from her winter hiding
To lie her length in the rain of early summer?
Who cut the leaf-buds open? What new-comer
Told the tall heron the place of her abiding?

Someone has been here:
Not the rough, drunken wind who shouts and wanders,
Trampling the woodpath; neither dawn nor gloaming
Nor the young airs in cowslip-garlands roaming.
Who was it then? The muted spirit ponders.

Close by the water
Wrapt in a dream, I saw a faint reflection
Like a wayfarer, calm and worn of features,
Clad in the brown of leaves and little creatures,
Stern as the moorland, russet of complexion.

Dark in the shadow
Fathomless eyes met mine with thought unspoken,
Wistful, yet deep within them laughter lingered.
With sunburnt hands a wooden flute he fingered
Under the thorn-tree, where the lights are broken.

Then the green river
Dimmed like a misted mirror; blossom only
Whitened it, on the covert water lying.
Westward along the willows ran a sighing.
Herd-like the clouds went home and left me lonely.

Over the meadows
Wild music came like spray upon the shingle;
Piping the world to mating; changing, calling
Low to the heart like doves when rain is falling.
Surely he cut his flute in Calvary's dingle?

I rose and followed
Right to the sunset-bars, yet never found him.
Backward along the edge of night returning
Sadly, I watched the slip of moon upburning
Silver, as if she drank the life around him.

In the dark aspens
Hark! a flute note; so still he's at his playing.
Tawny the furrows lie - his homely vesture.
Labourers pass: I see his very gesture -
Vigorous, tranquil, with his music straying.

Now I know surely
Who set the birds a-fire and touched the grasses -
Silent, without a footprint, no shade throwing.
Infinite worlds his shadow: all things growing
Stir with his breathing, follow as he passes.

LMC.

THE LITTLE SORROW

Within my heart a little sorrow crept
 And wept and wept.
Below the lilt of happiest melodies
 I heard its sighs
And cried: You little alien in my heart,
 Depart. Depart!

When suddenly a shadow crossed the floor
 And through the door
The Tragic Herald passed
 And blew a blast
Which drowned all music and made loud the air
 With wild despair.

Amid the harsh, discordant sounds of fate
 I listening wait:
Not hoping that a song can reach my ear;
 But just to hear
The little weeping grief I once bade cease
 Would now be peace.

ALDER BUDS

On New Year's Day I set beside his bed
An alder branch, already bravely budded.
He smiled, but hardly cared to turn his head
And see how close the purple spheres were studded,
Wherein the April leaves lay slumbering.
He spoke of leaves that rustled by his pillows,
More golden-sweet than airs in summer willows.
I did not know he would not see the spring.

UNFINISHED EMBROIDERY

On that last night, embroidering by his bed,
I often paused, his loving smile to meet,
And hear the tender approving words he said: -
'Your work is very beautiful, my sweet!'

The embroidery stays unfinished; Life's design
Must yet be stitched. How can I raise my head -
And no smile there? Lest sudden tears of mine
Should stain the cloth, and dull the silver thread.

For when the work is spread before his eyes
It must not seem too sadly incomplete.
So he may smile and say in glad surprise,
'Your work is very beautiful, my sweet'.

HUNGER

Not for the dear things said do I weep now;
Not for your deeds of quiet love and duty
Does my heart freeze and starve since you endow
Cold death with beauty.

Just for the look of utter comprehension;
The dear gay laugh that only true hearts know;
For these I would from life's severe detention
Arise and go.

THE DIFFERENCE

I walk among the daisies, as of old;
But he comes never more by lane or fold.
The same warm speedwell-field is dark with dew;
But he's away beyond a deeper blue.
A year today we saw the same flowers grow –
Last May! Last May! A century ago.

Above the speedwell leans the rosy tree
From which he plucked an apple bough for me.
Not all the blossom on the branches left
Can fill the place of that sweet bough bereft;
And none can fill the heart that loved him so
Last May! Last May! Eternities ago.

TREASURES

(FOR G.E.M.)

These are my treasures: just a word, a look,
A chiming sentence from his favourite book,
A large, blue, scented blossom that he found.
And plucked for me in some enchanted ground,
A joy he planned for us, a verse he made
Upon a birthday, the increasing shade
Of trees he planted by the waterside,
The echo of a laugh, his tender pride
In those he loved, his hand upon my hair,
The dear voice lifted in his evening prayer.

How safe they must be kept! So dear, so few,
And all I have to last my whole life through.
A silver mesh of loving words entwining,
At every crossing thread a tear-drop shining,
Shall close them in. Yet since my tears may break
The slender thread of brittle words, I'll make
A safer, humbler hiding-place apart,
And lock them in the fastness of my heart.

WINTER SUNRISE

All colours from the frozen earth have died,
And only shadow stains the cold, white snow:
But in the air the April tints abide;
Intangibly and radiantly they grow.
There bloom immortal crocuses, beside
A live-rose hedge, and irises that grow
Along a far green inlet - circling wide
Anemone fields where none but stars may go.
The ardours of a thousand springs are there;
Through infinite deeps they quicken, bright and tender:
In that sequestered garden of the air
No icy pall is heavy on the splendour.
Since you are not in the wintry world to love me,
How softly painted flushes Death above me!

'The spring of joy! The spring of joy! I have not found it.'
So my soul questioned and complained each day.
I asked the singing thrushes where it lay;
They cried - 'We never built or sang around it.'
I questioned of a harper, passing by
To a festival;
He said - 'I know of no such spring at all.'
This my soul heard, and wept most bitterly.
We wandered hand in hand
By many towns and hamlets, weary-hearted:
For those we questioned could not understand,
Or else they smiled in silence, and departed.
But, when the sun
Had left us in the dusk, mysteriously
Came One,
Who stood and called my weeping soul, and she
Unclasped her hand from mine and ran from me
Like a blown leaf to shelter. Kneeling low -
'The spring of joy!' I heard her say;
'Oh, great Wayfarer of the world, you know -
Let me know too - the way.'
I did not hear their colloquy, for they
Were both withdrawn from me;
But when she came again, as one who brings
A treasure, she was carrying tenderly
Some little rosy things
Like seeds. 'We go to plant sweet love,' she said,
'In pain's deep forest.' Then she pointed where
The dark trees loomed. I cried - 'Oh, soul - not so!
No spring of joy is there.'

She answered - 'None the less, at dawn we go.'
Like wraiths among the heavy shadows speeding,
Through trees as dark as night, as dumb as death,
We travelled, my soul leading.
Afraid at every breath,
When she stooped oftentimes to plant a seed,
I whispered - 'Speed, oh speed!
This place is wild and evil, full of harm.'
And yet she trembled not, but, gravely calm,
She said - 'There will be so much less to fear
For others, since the way that was so drear
Will be afire with flowers where we have been.'
But still she wept, and murmured wistfully -
'I thought today that we should both have seen
The lovely spring of joy!' Then carefully
She planted love's last seed, and we passed on.
And there, at the edge of the forest, gleamed and shone
A little rocky, rose-encircled spring,
So fair, so fresh, its music made us sing.
And One
(Oh, marvel!) held a cup for us, and said -
'I knew that dark way led
Straight here. Come, stand in the sun
And share with me.'
Then my soul knelt, and I,
Among the white and glistening flowers around it,
And drank the vital water with ecstasy -
So glad because through grief and love we found it,
The spring of joy!

This ~~little~~ heap of shivered
green ~~glass~~
That was a goblet, never wine
canned
Again, for that one note so sweet
Which only ~~could~~ can dissolve it, ~~o string care~~
The silence, ~~this lured~~ along
the delicate, ~~brittle~~ ~~thing~~
~~Being~~.
Besieged ~~with~~ beauty, made
~~truly~~ ~~ring~~
Shuddered, ~~& shandy~~
~~& shiver~~ ~~crick~~
fell inwards ~~better~~
as it ~~somehow~~,
~~the heavens might break~~ ~~you~~
food resounded.

Draft of 'The Goblet'

EARLY POEMS TO HENRY B. L. WEBB

(before and after their marriage, 12 June, 1912)

REFLECTIONS

No beauty is mine, and yet I saw today
A lovely face within my mirror glassed;
For you had looked upon me as you passed,
And still there lingered, as you went away,
Reflections of your grace in mouth and eye -
Like those rare dawns that paint the eastern sky
And mirror forth
Their beauty even in the hueless north.

ALONE

The lonely cuckoo calls
With a long hollow sound among the rocks
Of sun-touched sandstone, and the echo falls
Between the straight red pines to me, and knocks
Upon my heart again and yet again.
It thrills me
With some mysterious mingled joy and pain
That slumbers in the echoing refrain
And stills me.

If only you were here,
We'd go together through the buckler-fern
And watch the nuthatch climbing to his dear;
Then - so that you might follow - I would turn,
And, smiling, mount the steep, and leaning so
Above you,
Await your laughing kiss with eyes a-glow.
Ah! foolish dream - you do not even know
I love you.

THE GOBLET

This heap of shivered green and gold
That was a goblet, never wine can hold
Again, for that one note so sweet and strong
Which only could dissolve it, came along
The silence, and the delicate, brittle thing
Besieged by beauty, made to ring and ring,
Shuddered, and fell inwards, melted as it sounded,
As the heavens might break if the Voice of God resounded.
Ah! such a note your heart has sung to mine -
See how it breaks and spills its pride like wine.

LILIES IN THE VALLEYS

'Gather me lilies in the darkling valleys,
Gather me lilies in the valleys of delight!'
'How can I gather lilies with no cloak to cover me,
And no shoes for stony ways, and it the dark night?'
'I will give you shoes of silver and a cloak for rainy weather,
I will set you in a love that laughs and a love that grieves;
I'll hold you and I'll fold you and we'll travel down together
Where the lilies shine like seed-pearls in the wet, dark leaves.
And we'll gather the brittle lilies in the flowery valley,
We'll bind them into sheaves in the valley of delight,
And up from mossy mountains shall spring the lilied morning
Like our love from the valley - from the valley of the night.'

ISOLDE

Safe in his arms, one moment I abide
Above the sinister waves. For him, for me
Dawns a brief peace, a fleet eternity.
Our silence drowns the full and threatening tide,
And we forget how many loves have died,
How stealthy comes the dark and ebbing sea,
When one, arms empty, calls on vacancy
And hears the echoes mock on every side.

How brief is our warm joy, how soon to end!
Let us hold close and spend our interval
In heaven! But busy stranger, eager friend
Break in, and - never knowing - steal our all.
Then, even as a cynic fate denies
Our love, the bitter surf is in our eyes.

Beyond the darkling sea if no fair shore
Lies, where low flutes play, where the bitter surf
Is all forgotten, and the deep sea roar;
Behind the towering, granite hill of death
If no green crown of smooth, untrodden turf
Welcomes us where the long-lashed daisies eye
The sun so ardently they cannot die,
And the wind sleeps beneath the orchard breath:

Then not for us the fugitive and fond
Dream of a following music, harmonies
Made from the human discord; for beyond
Is mist, and a voice crying – <u>All is over</u>!
Here is our heaven, in one another's eyes,
In children's silver laughter. Here and now
Ripe scarlet apples bend the golden bough,
The bees' low roar is in the purple clover.

HUMBLE FOLK

Above our lane two rows of larches lean,
And lissom, rosy pines with wild black hair -
One slim, bright-fingered chestnut in between.
In blossom-time and berry-time and snow
Are muffled sounds of feet that come and go
Forever, from the cones and falling spines
And the sad, homeless rhythm of the pines.
These are our friends; we feel the griefs they bear;
We know the larches' thin young April song;
The heavy, dark endeavour of the cone
That goes alone
Among the thick, obliterating dust -
Impelled by something faint and strong
Within her, by the lust
Of death, towards the red and living tree.
Our fingers and the chestnut's touch and hold
The blue light and the gold,
And in a little drop them listlessly.
We know so few things more than these -
The larch that moans in rain
And every March puts roses on again;
The wise, mute chestnut listening to the bees;
The pine
That drinks the icy wind like wine.
We ask no better birth than their brown roots;
We dare not dream of immortality
Unshared by their brown fruits.
And when the wild bee's voice
Grows faint for us, we only ask to lie
Like two straight trees cut down together,
Not fearing any weather,
Too soundly sleeping even to rejoice.

Before his coming thunder breaks;
In plunging fires his way he takes;
Beneath his feet the daisies die,
And night looms darkly in his eye.
 So let him come!
 Let every silver, trilling bird be dumb!
 Let the white daisies drooping lie
 Crushed by his pitiless urgency.

He gives no soft or honied kiss,
Nor sings melodious rhapsodies
Of easy joy and bright reward:
His beauty is a flaming sword.
 So let him come!
 Let every silver, trilling bird be dumb!
 Let the white daisies drooping lie
 Crushed by his pitiless urgency.

'BE STILL, YOU LITTLE LEAVES'

Be still, you little leaves! nor tell your sorrow
To any passing bat or hovering owl
Or the low-splashing, restless water-fowl.
You flowering rushes, sigh not till tomorrow;
Come not, sad wind, out of your caverns eerie:
My love is sleeping, and my love is weary.

From the Devil's Chair

Gladys Mary Coles

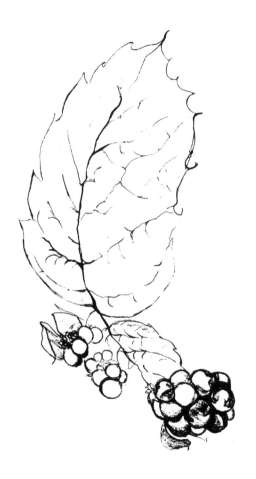

L.M.C.

THE HAPPY LIFE

No silks have I, no furs nor feathers,
But one old gown that knows all weathers;
No veils nor parasols nor lace,
But rough hands and a tanned face.
Yet the soft, crinkled leaves are mine
Where pale, mysterious veins shine,
And laced larches upon the blue,
And grey veils where the moon looks through;
The cries of birds across the lawns
In dark and teeming April dawns;
The sound of wings at the door-sill,
Where grows the wet-eyed tormentil;
The ripe berry's witcheries –
Its perfect round that satisfies;
And the gay scent of the wood I burn,
And the slap of butter in a busy churn.

K. Coles

Who'll walk the fields with us to town,
In an old coat and a faded gown?
We take our roots and country sweets
Where high walls shade the steep old streets,
And golden bells and silver chimes
Ring up and down the sleepy times.
The morning mountains smoke like fires;
The sun spreads out his shining wires;
The mower in the half-mown leasur
Sips his tea and takes his pleasure.
Along the lanes slow waggons amble;
The sad-eyed calves awake and gamble;
The foal that lay so sorrowful
Is playing in the grasses cool.
By slanting ways, in slanting sun,
Through startled lapwings now we run
Along the pale green hazel-path,
Through April's lingering aftermath
Of lady's smock and lady's slipper;
We stay to watch a nesting dipper.
The rabbits eye us while we pass,
Out of the sorrel-crimson grass;
The blackbird sings, without a fear,
Where honeysuckle horns blow clear –
Cool ivory stained with true vermilion;
And here, within a silk pavilion,
Small caterpillars lie at ease,
The endless shadows of the trees
Are painted purple and cobalt;

Grandiloquent, the rook-files halt,
Each one aware of you and me,
And full of conscious dignity.
Our shoes are golden as we pass
With pollen from the pansied grass.
Beneath an elder - set anew
With large clean plates to catch the dew -
On fine white cheese and bread we dine:
The clear brook-water tastes like wine.
If all folk lived with labour sweet
Of their own busy hands and feet,
Such marketing, it seems to me,
Would make an end of poverty.

THE LITTLE HILL

This is the hill, ringed by the misty shire -
The mossy, southern hill,
The little hill where larches climb so high.
Among the stars aslant
They chant;
Along the purple lower slopes they lie
In lazy golden smoke, more faint, more still
Than the pale woodsmoke of the cottage fire.
Here some calm Presence takes me by the hand
And all my heart is lifted by the chant
Of them that lean aslant
In golden smoke and sing, and softly bend:
And out from every larch-bole steals a friend.

FREEDOM

When on the moss-green hill the wandering wind
Drowses, and lays his brazen trumpet down,
When snow-fed waters gurgle, cold and brown,
And wintered birds creep from the stacks to find
Solace, while each bright eye begins to see
A visionary nest in every tree -
Let us away, out of the murky day
Of sullen towns, into the silver noise
Of woods where every bud has found her way
Sunward, and every leaf has found a voice.

THE SECRET JOY

Face to face with the sunflower,
Cheek to cheek with the rose,
We follow a secret highway
Hardly a traveller knows.
The gold that lies in the folded bloom
Is all our wealth;
We eat of the heart of the forest
With innocent stealth.
We know the ancient roads
In the leaf of a nettle,
And bathe in the blue profound
Of a speedwell petal.

THE WILD ROSE

Five pointed sepals with a pearly sheen
Uphold the frail cup's curved transparency,
White-veined below, and flushing tenderly
Towards the brim. A shadow lies between
Each loose-curved petal, and the scent - so keen,
So sweet - is very wine of joy to me.
The humming honey-people eagerly
Enjoy this loving-cup among the green.
We share together, the butterfly, the bee
And I, and the little beetles that gleam and shine.
And yet one more, my spirit whisperingly
Has spoken of, whose banquet is divine.
Deep down within the chalice I can see
The gold He left there as His kingly fee.

Elves of the hollow and the dewpond still,
Take pity! Gather for me dew as chill
As ice, and glittering-pure as early dawn,
From pink-tipped daisies on the printless lawn
And the transparent cups of apple-bloom,
And lily bells, to save me from this doom
Of being so brown!
Bring me an unguent made of scented roots;
Pomander of green herbs and scarlet fruits,
Verbena leaves, mallow and melilot,
And balmy rosemary, that I may not
Be brown!
O sweet wild rose,
You have so fair a colour in your face!
Spare me a blush; take from me this disgrace
Of being so brown!
Lilies, you do not guess,
In your pale loveliness,
The grief it is to hear,
In a voice dispassionate and clear,
'You're very brown!'

THE GARDEN IN WINTER

The winter sun that rises near the south
Looks coldly on my garden of cold clay;
Like some old dotard with a bitter mouth,
Shrugs his grey robe to his ears and creeps away.
Come down the mountains, April! with young eyes,
And roguish daisy-children trooping after,
Draw from the sullen clay red peonies,
Bring back the sun as a stripling full of laughter!

SNOWDROP TIME

Ah, hush! Tread softly through the rime,
For there will be a blackbird singing, or a thrush.
Like coloured beads the elm-buds flush:
All the trees dream of leaves and flowers and light.
And see! The northern bank is much more white
Than frosty grass, for now is snowdrop time.

AN OLD WOMAN

They bring her flowers - red roses heavily sweet,
White pinks and Mary-lilies and a haze
Of fresh green ferns; around her head and feet
They heap more flowers than she in all her days
Possessed. She sighed once - 'Posies aren't for me;
They cost too much.'
Yet now she sleeps in them, and cannot see
Or smell or touch.

Now in a new and ample gown she lies -
White as a daisy-bud, as soft and warm
As those she often saw with longing eyes,
Passing some bright shop window in a storm.
Then, when her flesh could feel, how harsh her wear!
Not warm nor white.
This would have pleased her once. She does not care
At all tonight.

They give her tears - affection's frailest flowers -
And fold her close in praise and tenderness:
She does not heed. Yet in those empty hours
If there had come, to cheer her loneliness,
But one red rose in youth's rose-loving day,
A smile, a tear,
It had been good. But now she goes her way
And does not hear.

HILL PASTURES

High on the hill the curlews and the whimbrels,
Go mating all day long with a sweet whistle;
With a sound of chiming bells and shaken timbrels,
And silver rings that fall in a crystal cup.
They laugh, as lovers laugh when the moon is up,
Over the cotton-grass and the carline thistle.

Poised in his airy spiral the snipe is calling,
Summoning love with a music mournful and lonely
As a lost lamb in the night, rising, falling,
Stranger than any melody, wilder than song.
He cries of life that is short, and death that is long
Telling his dusky love to one heart only.

Once in seven days a plaintive ringing
Sounds from the little chapel high in the heather,
Out with the sorrowful snipe and the whimbrel winging
The wild hill ponies hear it there as they graze,
And whinny, and call to their foals, and stand at gaze
Hearing a clear voice in the clear weather.

And out of pine-dark farms and windy places,
And quiet cottages low in the valley hiding,
Brown folk come with still and wistful faces.
Straying by twos and threes, like the peaceful sheep,
Into the small brown shippen of souls they creep,
Seeking a calm like the hills', but more abiding.

The scarlet-jewelled ashtree sighed - 'He cometh,
For whom no wine is poured and no bee hummeth.'

The huddled bean-sheaves under the moon,
Like black tents, will be vanished soon.
So fast the days draw in and are over,
So early the bees are gone from the clover -
Today, tomorrow -
And nights are dark, and as cold as sorrow.

He's gone, her man, so good with his hands
In the harvest field and the lambing shed.
Straight ran his share in the deep ploughlands -
And now he marches among the dead.

The ash let fall her gems, and moaned - 'He cometh,
And no bee hummeth.'

'O children, come in from your soldier-play
In the black bean tents! The night is falling;
Owls with their shuddering cry are calling;
A dog howls, lonely, far away.'

His son comes in like a ghost through the door.
He'll be ready, maybe, for the next big war.

O world, come in from the leasowes grey
And cold, where swaths of men are lying,
And horror to shuddering horror crying!
Come home
To the wisdom of those that till the loam,
And give man time for his working-day!

Then the white-blossomed ash will sing - 'He cometh,
For whom the loving-cup is poured, the wild bee hummeth.'

THE LAD OUT THERE

Oh, Powers of Love, if still you lean
Above a world so black with hate,
Where yet - as it has ever been -
The loving heart is desolate,
Look down upon the lad I love,
(My brave lad, tramping through the mire) -
Light Thou the stars for him above!
Now nights are dark and mornings dim,
Let him in his long watching know
That I too count the minutes slow
And light the lamp of love for him.
The sight of death, the sleep forlorn,
The old homesickness vast and dumb -
Amid these things, so bravely borne,
Let my long thoughts about him come.
I see him in the weary file;
So young he is, so dear to me,
With ever ready sympathy
And wistful eyes and cheerful smile.
However far he travels on,
Thought follows, like the willow-wren
That flies the stormy seas again
To lands where her delight is gone.
Whatever he may be or do
While absent far beyond my call,
Bring him, the long day's march being through,
Safe home to me some evenfall!

TO MY DEAR

I give you laughing names,dear, for I see
Tears like a sea stand up before the sun,
And the whole world grown dark with tragedy,
And life cut off before the laugh is done.

THE PLOVERS

The plovers are shrill tonight,
For the moon is urgent with them, and silence presses
Close on their brains, on their round wings molten-white
That cleave through light into further wildernesses of light

A NIGHT SKY (1916)

The moon, beyond her violet bars,
From towering heights of thunder-cloud,
Sheds calm upon our scarlet wars,
To soothe a world so small, so loud.
And little clouds like feathered spray,
Like rounded waves on summer seas,
Or frosted panes on a winter day,
Float in the dark blue silences.
Within their foam, transparent, white,
Like flashing fish the stars go by
Without a sound across the night.
In quietude and secrecy
The white, soft lightnings feel their way
To the boundless dark and back again,
With less stir than a gnat makes
In its little joy, its little pain.

AN ESTRAY (1916)

How did I come so low,
Wandering here
Under clouds of wrath and woe
With a heart full of fear?

How did I chance to roam
Into the night,
Away from my delicate home
Of colour and light?

Out of a land serene,
Airy and lone,
I strayed to the sadness terrene,
To a people of stone.

Ah, my soul is afraid,
Homesick, estranged.
I long for my palace of jade
And the forest I ranged.

'LIKE A POPPY ON A TOWER'

Like a poppy on a tower
The present hour!
The wind stirs, the wind awakes,
Beneath its feet the tower shakes.
All down the crannied wall
Torn scarlet petals fall,
Like scattered fire or shivered glass
And drifting with their motion pass
Torn petals of blue shadow
From the grey tower to the green meadow.

THE DOOR

I heard humanity, through all the years,
Wailing, and beating on a dark, vast door
With urgent hands and eyes blinded by tears.
Will none come forth to them for evermore?
Like children at their father's door, who wait,
Crying 'Let us in!' on some bright birthday morn,
Quite sure of joy, they grow disconsolate,
Left in the cold unanswered and forlorn.
Forgetting even their toys in their alarms,
They only long to climb on father's bed
And cry their terrors out in father's arms.
And maybe, all the while, their father's dead.

THE FLOCKMASTER (1916)

I come
Out of the heart of night, where calm distils
Like dew in the helleborine.
Forever the sheep have known me, straitened and dumb
In their life like a dark ravine;
They clamour of me to the empty sky and the hills;
They cry with a great homesickness under the moon
For something they know and know not, within them, beyond
That they feel when I dwell on the slope in the heat of n
That they taste in the cold dew-pond.
Only a little less of me have they known
Than the poet knows, and far as he they have wandered
With their lambs, on the clear skyline like shadows steal
Clad in the fleece of their crying,
Following me on whom all creatures have pondered -
Inarticulate, sighing
After the half-revealed, the unrevealing,
The shepherd who dwelleth alone.

K. COLES

SUNSET

Dull is the sun as an old lanthorn guttering,
And wild the valleys where the coughing sheep,
With wool torn by the brambles, climb and leap.
Here on the hill-top the old wind is uttering
His ancient, weary, unassuaged complaints,
Baying among the rocks that rise like tombs;
Shouting aloud the wild and secret dooms
Of all things living, while the evening faints
Amid the torn white flocks of cloud that fly
In panic all across the western sky.

A FACTORY OF PEACE

I watched him in the loud and shadowy lane
Of life; and every face that passed him by
Grew bright and restful, smiling inwardly,
As though he gave for all their grief and pain
Largesse of quiet, soft as summer rain,
And balsam tinctured with tranquillity.
Yet his own eyes were dark with agony.
'O herbalist,' I cried, 'in that calm brain
What tortured thing is moaning while you heal?'
He said — 'Where balms are made for human uses,
Red furnace-fires and wheel on grinding wheel
Must crush and purify the crude herb-juices.
Within some hearts the conflict cannot cease:
They are the sick world's factories of peace.'

LATER   POEMS

THE MESSENGER

As a pale moth passes
In the April grasses,
So I come and go
Softlier than snow.
Swifter than a star
Through the heart I flee,
Singing things that are
And things that cannot be.
I whisper to the mole,
And the cold fish in the sea,
And to man's wistful soul
Life sendeth me.
As a grey moth passes
Through October grasses
So I come and go,
Softlier than snow.

THE SPIRIT OF EARTH

Love me – and I will give into your hands
The rare, enamelled jewels of my lands,
Flowers red and blue,
Tender with air and dew.

From far green armouries of pools and meres
I'll reach for you my lucent sheaves of spears –
The singing falls,
Where the lone ousel calls.

When, like a passing light upon the sea,
Your wood-bird soul shall clap her wings and flee,
She shall but nest
More closely in my breast.

K.C.

IN APRIL

In April, in April
My heart is set
Where the pansy and the violet
And the daffodil,
And close-folded lilies grow
In borders dark with melted snow.
Wakening there from wintry sleep
With every bud I sunward creep.
The empurpled crocuses, that dare
With delicate veins the dawn-cold air,
Cradle me in their chalices
Amid the golden sediment.
There I lie in warm content
And listen to the velvet bees,
Watching their dark blue shadows fall
Along the half-transparent wall.
When the sharp-pointed grasses prick
Upward, all passionate to be free,
I share their conflict, fierce and quick,
With the earthen will; I know their glee.
In the star-tinted pimpernel
I hear the silver tongue of rain;
And learn the perfume thrushes smell,
Which makes their song as keen as pain;
And see, where long-lashed daisies crowd,
New revelations in the cloud.
That is why, when old I grow
And near my end, I shall not know.
For every year my heart is set

With the pansy and the violet
And the daffodil:
Submerged within their beauty, I
Transcend my poor mortality.

There is a presence on the lonely hill,
Lovely and chill:
There is an emanation in the wood,
Half understood.
They come upon me like an evening cloud,
Stranger than moon-rise, whiter than a shroud.
I shall not see them plain
Ever again,
Though in my childhood days
I knew their ways.
They are as secret as the black cloud-shadows
Sliding along the ripe midsummer grass;
With a breath-taking majesty they pass,
Down by the water in the mournful meadows;
Out of the pale pink distance at the falling
Of dusk they gaze - remote, summoning, chill;
Sweetly in April I have heard them calling
Where through black ash-buds gleams the purple hill

SPRING IN THE WEST

Soon amid the inviolable places
Will green, rustling steeples chime again
With the sweet, glassy bell-notes of the wren.
Soon the plain shall lie beneath blue spaces -
Bold and broad and ruddy in the sun,
Long and lean to the moon when day is done.

Soon will come the strange, heart-lifting season
When through the dark, still dawns, where nothing was,
Steals the mysterious whisper of growing grass;
And a joy like pain possesses the soul, without reason,
Between the budding of day and the lapse of night,
With the clear, cold scent of wet starlight.

GREEN RAIN

Into the scented woods we'll go
And see the blackthorn swim in snow.
High above, in the budding leaves,
A brooding dove awakes and grieves;
The glades with mingled music stir,
And wildly laughs the woodpecker.
When blackthorn petals pearl the breeze,
There are the twisted hawthorn trees
Thick-set with buds, as clear and pale
As golden water or green hail -
As if a storm of rain had stood
Enchanted in the thorny wood,
And, hearing fairy voices call,
Hung poised, forgetting how to fall.

THE ANCIENT GODS

Certainly there were splashings in the water,
Certainly there were shadows on the hill,
Dark with the leaves of purple-spotted orchis;
But now all's still.

It may be that the catkin-covered sallow,
With her illusive, glimmering surprise,
Pale golden-tinted as a tall young goddess,
Deceived my eyes;

And the white birches wading in the margin,
Each one a naked and a radiant god,
Dazzled me; and the foam was flung by currents
Where no feet trod.

Only I know I saw them - stately, comely,
Within the leafy shadows of the stream;
They woke amid the shallow, singing water
A fading gleam.

They left no trail for any beast to follow,
No track upon the moss for man to trace;
In a long, silent file up-stream they vanished
With measured pace.

The hollow water curved about their ankles
Like amber; splashes glistened on their thighs;
Sun barred their lifted heads and their far-seei
Yet sightless eyes.

Some were like women, with deep hair of willows,
Bare breasts and gracious arms and long, smooth hips,
And the red roses of desire half frozen
Upon their lips:

But most were massive-browed and massive-shouldered
And taller than the common height of men.
They went as those that have not home nor kindred,
Nor come again.

Still, where the birches fingered their reflection,
The thrushes chanted to the evening sky;
Still the grey wag-tails raced across the shingle
As they went by.

Beyond the furthest of the saffron shallows
I lost them in the larches' rainy green,
And only saw the stretches of marsh-mallows
Where they had been.

You say the sallow and the birch deceived me:
But I know well that I beheld today
The ancient gods, unheralded, majestic,
Upon their way.

A HAWTHORN BERRY

How sweet a thought,
How strange a deed,
To house such glory in a seed –
A berry, shining rufously,
Like scarlet coral in the sea!
A berry, rounder than a ring,
So round, it harbours everything;
So red, that all the blood of men
Could never paint it so again.
And, as I hold it in my hand,
A fragrance steals across the land:
Rich, on the wintry heaven, I see
A white, immortal hawthorn-tree.

IN DARK WEATHER

Against the gaunt, brown-purple hill
The bright brown oak is wide and bare;
A pale-brown flock is feeding there -
    Contented, still.

No bracken lights the bleak hill-side;
No leaves are on the branches wide;
No lambs across the fields have cried;
    - Not yet.

But whorl by whorl the green fronds climb;
The ewes are patient till their time;
The warm buds swell beneath the rime -
    For life does not forget.

THE PLAIN IN AUTUMN

A solemn land of long-fulfilled desires
Is this, and year by year the self-same fires
Burn in the trees. The untarnished colours keep
The sweetness of the young earth's infant sleep:
Beyond the plain, beneath the evening star,
The burnished hills like stately peacocks are.
Great storms march out. The flocks across the grass
Make their low plaint while the swift shadows pass:
Memoried deep in Hybla, the wild bee
Sings in the purple-fruited damson tree:
And, darkly sweet as Ruth, the dairy maid
By the lean, laughing shepherd is waylaid.

Virocon – Virocon –
Still the ancient name rings on
And brings, in the untrampled wheat,
The tumult of a thousand feet.

Where trumpets rang and men marched by,
None passes but the dragon-fly.
Athwart the grassy town, forlorn,
The lone dor-beetle blows his horn.

The poppy standards droop and fall
Above one rent and mournful wall:
In every sunset-flame it burns,
Yet towers unscathed when day returns.

And still the breaking seas of grain
Flow havenless across the plain:
The years wash on, their spindrift leaps
Where the old city, dreaming, sleeps.

Grief lingers here, like mists that lie
Across the dawns of ripe July;
On capital and corridor
The pathos of the conqueror.

The pillars stand, with alien grace,
In churches of a younger race;
The chiselled column, black and rough,
Becomes a roadside cattle-trough:

The skulls of men who, right or wrong,
Still wore the splendour of the strong,
Are shepherds' lanterns now, and shield
Their candles in the lambing field.

But when, through evening's open door,
Two lovers tread the broken floor,
And the wild-apple petals fall
Round passion's scarlet festival;

When cuckoos call from the green gloom
Where dark, shelving forests loom;
When foxes bark beside the gate,
And the grey badger seeks his mate —

There haunts within them secretly
One that lives while empires die,
A shrineless god whose songs abide
Forever in the countryside.

THE WOOD

Tall, feathered birches, on the tides of air,
Wash to and fro, like seaweeds fine and fair,
And deep in leaf and blossom from all eyes
The rope-walk of the honeysuckle lies.
There, crimson foxgloves taper slenderly,
And the brown-seeded brake grows ten feet high.
There are strange, flaming toad-stools, and the berries
Of ash and rose, that shine like scarlet cherries.
The rose-bay willowherb, in her bridal hour,
Blooms, and the larch sets forth her rosy flower.
Kestrels are there, and tawny foxes play
Amid the shadows in the early day.
Low cry the sheep, and leave their shining fleece
On the long vines of purple blackberries.
High in their minstrel gallery above,
Hidden in fretted leaves, dove answers dove,
And like a distant bell, melodiously
Haunting these glades, the music of the bee
Chimes all the summer. ...Like a bird, with wings
Dusky and silent, I would flit through spring's
Wistful, immaculate colours; through the dream
And hush of summer; down the rush and gleam
Of autumn; and when winter, with a moan,
Swept through the freezing wood aloof, alone,
Prisoning the pine needles in shining, hollow
Cases of ice, yet the brown bird would follow.
Light as a last year's leaf I'd flutter by,
With the sad note of finches in July.

Still should the foxgloves gather, spring by spring;
Still should the feathered birches wash and swing
Upon the tides of air, and in the sun
Each autumn should the little foxes run,
While I in shadow dwelt. Dark on the sky
Should kestrels anchor, watching warily
For small brown birds: but in the meadow green
I'd fearless flit, beneath their gaze unseen.

MY OWN TOWN

In this old town I know so well
I have dwelt in heaven and in hell,
And seen its folk go to and fro
With faces of unthinkable woe,
Ferocious as primaeval beasts,
Or rapt as angels at their feasts,
When close they press in silver rows
While up and down the chalice goes,
Made of a sapphire, filled to the brim
With God. I have seen them walk like kings
Pondering on majestic things.
And where the gossip gables lean
Chatting, I've met with faces mean
With meanness past all grace or cure.
As long as those blue hills endure,
That stand around the gracious plain
Which circles-in the town, and rain
Marches across the corn, and tears
Weigh down the harvest of our years,
So long what I have seen and felt,
When in its churches I have knelt
And wandered by the evening stream
And seen the April roadways gleam,
Shall live. And when the traffic's hum
Is gone, the busy market dumb
As a winter bee, and all the spires
Are melted in the hungry fires
Of Time, and not a house remains –
Then here, upon the empty plains,

Encircled by the changeless heights,
As changeless through the days and nights
As they, in colours that cannot fade,
Shall stand the town that I have made
With golden house and silver steeple
And a strange uplifted people,
Who in their charmed streets shall go
Hushed with a tremendous woe
And a joy as deep and vast
As shadows that the mountains cast.
And I shall dwell where once unknown
I passed, and all shall be my own,
Because I built of joy and tears
A city that defies the years.

THE NEIGHBOUR'S CHILDREN

They run to meet me, clinging to my dress,
The neighbour's children. With a wild unrest
And sobbings of a strange, fierce tenderness,
I snatch them to my breast.
But my baby, ah! my baby
Weepeth — weepeth
In the far loneliness of nonentity,
And holds his little spirit hands to me,
Crying 'Mother!' and nearer creepeth;
Beats on my heart's lit window anxiously,
Shivering and sobbing, 'Mother, let me in!
Give me my rosy dress, my delicate dress
Of apple-blossom flesh, dark eyes like flowers,
And warm mouth kissed by a red anemone.
Give me my toys — the hills, the seas, the sun,
Loud song, wild winds, the morning's cloudy towers.
Give hands to hold and ears to hear and feet to run.
Give me my lesson books — fear, love and sin —
All hell to brave, all heaven to win!'
Then, shadowy, wild and wan,
A little face peers in,
Except in dreams unknown even to me,
And like a summer cloud is gone.
It is the neighbour's children, playing near,
With voices ringing clear.
But far in twilight, like a moon-awakened bird,
Was that another, fainter laugh I heard?

And so, Anne Everard, in those leafy Junes
Long withered; in those ancient, dark Decembers,
Deep in the drift of time, haunted by tunes
Long silent; you, beside the homely embers,
Or in some garden fragrant and precise
Were diligent and attentive all day long!
Fashioning with bright wool and stitches nice
Your sampler, did you hear the thrushes' song
Wistfully? While, in orderly array,
Six rounded trees grew up; the alphabet,
Stout and uncompromising, done in grey;
The Lord's Prayer, and your age, in violet;
Did you, Anne Everard, dream from hour to hour
How the young wind was crying on the hill,
And the young world was breaking into flower?
With small head meekly bent, all mute and still,
Earnest to win the promised great reward,
Did you not see the birds, at shadow-time,
Come hopping all across the dewy sward?
Did you not hear the bells of Faery chime
Liquidly, where the brittle hyacinths grew?
Your dream - attention; diligence, your aim!
And when the last long needleful was through,
When, laboured for so long, the guerdon came -
Thomson, his Seasons, neatly bound in green -
How brightly would the golden letters shine!
Ah! many a petalled May the moon has seen
Since Anne - attentive, diligent, aetat nine -
Puckering her young brow, read the stately phrases.

Sampler and book are here without a stain –
Only Anne Everard lies beneath the daisies;
Only Anne Everard will not come again.

GOING FOR THE MILK

Going for the milk –
A toddling child with skin like curds,
On a May morning in a charm of birds:

Going for the milk
With laughing, teasing lads, at seventeen,
With rosy cheeks and breast as soft as silk –
Eh! what a mort of years between!

Going for the milk
Through my Jim's garden, past the bush o' balm,
With my first baby sleeping on my arm:

It's fifty year, come Easter, since that day;
The work'us ward is cold, my eyes be dim;
Never no more I'll go the flowery way,
Fetching the milk. I drink the pauper's skim,
And mind me of those summer days, and Jim
Telling me as my breast was soft as silk –
And that first day I missed to fetch the milk.

TO G.D.M.

I see you stand, a sturdy little lad
In your new suit, the sunlight on your head,
Watching the camera with your earnest eyes;
For thence would come (the photographer had said)
For good boys, sweets. But soon your eyes grew sad,
And soon you frowned in puzzled, pained surprise.
You had been so good a boy, quite free from blame,
Yet from the obstinate camera no sweets came!

In such an hour, so bitterly deceived,
Did it comfort you that one stood by and grieved?
Someone who thought the sweets well-earned, and knew
Whoever was in fault, it was not you.

THE WATCHER

Where the black woods grow sparse and die,
A giant broods against the sky.
The storm his chlamys, and his head
Bent to the spirits of the dead.

The windhover, floating like a leaf,
Passes him safely, clear of grief.
The auburn doves within the wood
Have pondered him and understood.

The wandering breaths of cattle come
Towards his fastness, and the hum
From paper homes of wasps, and cries
Of bees in their refectories.

The evening smoke ascends again
Out of the sapphire-circled plain,
And to the oatfield, pale as wax,
A black swift hurtles like an axe.

There shadow, with her gentle fingers,
Soothes all the dappled land; she lingers
On little croft and ample field,
With their benign and wistful yield.

The Watcher on the summit stands
With a blue goblet in his hands;
He slowly drinks the glimmering years,
The sparkling laughter and the tears.

He is not angered nor forgiving;
He does not sever dead from living,
But sees them all as long gone by,
Returning in futurity.

And still he counts, with stooping head,
The spirits of the living dead –
A soul or two in every field,
And in the furrowed, crimson weald;

And some in every orchard-close,
Who pruned the cherry and the rose,
And waited for the damson sweet,
And plodded through the brittle wheat.

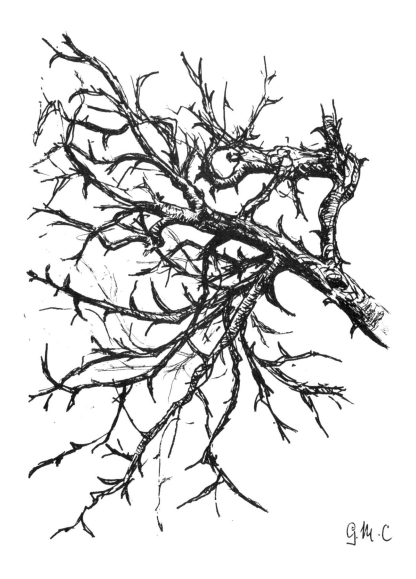

NOVEMBER

When on my merry garden cold fogs rise
And from these golden trees the blossoms fall;
When in the hollow, painted morning skies
No more the sweet birds call;
When music dies, and colour blurs to grey,
And laughter slips into a sob and fails;
When all my troops of dreams, serene and gay,
Are frozen nightingales –
Where shall I turn, since God is far withdrawn,
And heaven a palace fallen in the sea?
How can I live, a stranger to the dawn?
Ah, who will comfort me?
You, dear, with sadness of unflinching sight,
Behold the pitiful world, the pitiless sky,
Strong in the midst of storm and cold and night,
More great, more brave, than I;
And I could live with sorrow all my days,
Having your word of praise.

AUTUMN

When autumn winds are on the hill
    And darkly rides the wasting moon,
I creep within your arms, and still
    Am safe in the golden heart of June.

WINTER

If I should be the first to go away
Out of the golden sunlight of our peace,
When the dear sacrament of common day
And lowly, love-empurpled tasks shall cease;
When the old books beside the evening fire
Neglected lie, and closed the garden gate,
And from our hill the blossom-tinted shire
Gathers for us an air disconsolate -
Then, oh beloved! hold me close, so close,
Nearer than thought of pain or sad regret;
So wrapped in you, I even should forget
The lifelong dread of parting; and the rose
Of June would flower for me, though cold and slow
And weary on our roof-tree fell the snow.
Speak to me then with that most tender voice,
Wherein I hear the forest murmur fall,
The songs of the corn and velvet-throated doves
That each on each with muted music call,
Minding each other of their leafy loves.
So gathered safe within your voice, your eyes,
Your dear protecting smile, I shall not know
When the black frost sets in, the dark wind cries.
For as the squirrel and the mole, so warm
Within their snow-proof chambers, and the bee
Walled in with summer, wake not, though the storm
Besieges hive and forest - so with me
All will be well; for, sealed in dreamless slumbers,
I shall not know my world is desolate.
Ages may pass, like leaves that no man numbers,
While in the nest of love I hibernate.

WHY?

Why did you come, with your enkindled eyes
And mountain-look, across my lower way,
And take the vague dishonour from my day
By luring me from paltry things, to rise
And stand beside you, waiting wistfully
The looming of a larger destiny?

Why did you with strong fingers fling aside
The gates of possibility, and say
With vital voice the words I dream today?
Before, I was not much unsatisfied:
But since a god has touched me and departed,
I run through every temple, broken-hearted.

A FAREWELL

Beloved, once more I take the winter way
   Through solitude's dark mountains, purple and cold
As frozen pansies, toward my house of clay
   Where winds shall drink my tears, and shadows fold.

I dare not dwell so near to ecstasy
   Lest I grow reckless, seeing the dear, the good,
And so, beseeching for it childishly,
   Should spoil its beauty and my womanhood.

Yet will the breathless moments when you smiled,
   Looking upon me, haunt me. It is not well
Remembering, when winter floods are wild,
   Becalmed lilies and the summer's spell.

Farewell, beloved! Since you have grown too dear,
   I must be gone. I take my pilgrimage
In haste - so much I love you, so much fear.
   Wisdom may grow from tears, peace fall with age.

BEYOND

Far beyond, far beyond,
Deeper than the glassy pond,
My shivering spirit sits and weeps
And never sleeps.

Like the autumn dove that grieves,
Darkly hid in dove-like leaves,
So I moan within a woe
None may know.

ABSENCE

Beloved, I walk on the clear, bright grass.
Multiple-tinted, magical, still
Is the plain, where the blue cloud shadows pass,
The silver tree, the forget-me-not hill.

Gossamer-green are the pastures; there
The sheep cry loud and the sheep cry low.
Sounds of haymaking fill the air,
Fugitive voices come and go.

Surely this is the land of rest,
Safe at the hithermost end of sleep,
Where loud winds slumber and troubles cease,
Where no hands tremble and no eyes weep.

The clamour of rooks, with a peaceful sound,
Comes from the woodland far away,
Possessing the plain, from bound to bound,
With the dreamy life of a summer day.

I only am sad, my dear, my dear!
Though the delicate aspen shakes like a chime,
And the low hills, greener than glass, and clear,
Lead to the summits that fairies climb.

I care not for day, while linnet and swallow,
That have no sorrow, possess the sky;
I care not for night, when the dark blue hollow
Is full of stars for the white owl's eye.

Sad is the rose-red flower of the dawn,
And the smell of the hay in the tender dew;
I hear no sheep, nor birds on the lawn,
Because of my own voice calling you.

APPLE-BLOW

The apple-blow that was so sweet,
So pink and clear,
Has flung its petals at my feet,
My dear — my dear!

The petalled joys that made my crown
When you were here,
Like heavy tears are fallen down,
My dear — my dear!

The doves that coo in Colomen
Are never heard by mortal men
But when a human creature passes
Underneath the churchyard grasses.
In deep voices, velvet-warm,
They tell of ancient perils, storm
Long hushed, and hopes withered and dead,
And joys a long while harvested.

There was a lady small and thin
(Oh, grave! Why did you let her in?)
Her voice was sad as a dove's, her feet
Went softly through the yellow wheat,
Like stars that haunt the evening west.
Hers was the tall, round, sunny cote
Whence, as she called, her doves would float
Softly, on arm and shoulder rest,
Until the lady, leaning so,
Under the feathers of rose and snow,
Wing of azure and purple plume,
Was like a slim tree bent with bloom.

And still, at Colomen, they say,
When midsummer has stolen away
The last arch primrose, and swiftly fall
Hawthorn petals, wan as a pall,
And the grave blackbirds, that of late
Shouted the sun up, meditate,

You hear about the ruined cote
A mighty, muted sound of wings,
And faint, ghostly flutterings.
Then, if your death is near, you see
A lady standing like a tree
Bent down with blossom. Long ago
Her little joy, her long woe!

In an April dawn of rose and flame
A poor, travelling painter came
Through tasselled woods, and in the tower
Beheld the lady, like a flower -
A pale flower beneath the hill,
Trembling when the air is still,
Broken when the storms are wild.
The lady looked on him, and smiled.
Woe, woe to Colomen,
Where never lovers come again,
Laughing in the morning air!

Dew decked the lady's hair
Because the lilac, purple and tall,
Saw her beauty and let fall
All her silver, all her sweet.
In dove-grey dawns their lips would meet
In the room beneath the tower
Where the drowsy sunlight smote
Seldom, and the air would creep
Stealthily and half asleep,
While stillness held the dancing mote,
And croonings fell from the ivied cote
With a musical, low roar,
Like summer seas on a fairy shore.

The boding wind had moaned of loss;
The boding shadow laid a cross
From the barred window to their feet;
The doves made a heart-broken, sweet
Clamour of some eerie thing.
They did not hear nor understand
How soon love is withered away
Like a flower on a frosty day!

Early in a summer dawn
When the shadows of the doves were drawn
Down the roof, and from the clover
The bees' low roar came up, her lover
Finished her portrait, thin and small
And pale, with an ethereal
Sweet air,, because he had seen her soul
Come to the threshold when she stole
To meet him. There forever she stood
Like a silver fairy in a wood
Or a maytree in the moonlight.
He told her of his dream's delight,
How they would dwell alone, aloof,
With doves crooning on the roof.

He had painted through a sapphire June
Into a thunderous dark July.
Alas! How fleet is spring! How soon
From all their little windows fly
The doves of joy! In an evil hour
Her sister saw him leave the tower.

For all her simple country grace,
Hers was a haughty, lordly race.
When night was thick and black above,
They sent the press-gang for her love.

All day, beside the memoried cote
She lay so still they thought her dead,
Her doves, that wheeled above her head.
But in her eyes a wild, remote,
Inhuman sorrow slumbered.

When next the clover called the bee,
Where was she? Ah, where was she?

She dragged her leaden limbs across
The grey lawns, to hear the sound
That turned a sword within her wound
And made her agony of loss
So keen that if she held her breath
She almost heard the feet of death.

When all her thronging pigeons cooed
Around, with outspread arms she stood.
She seemed a pale and slender tree,
Bent with snow and not with bloom –
Bent lower towards the tomb.

She would be free of the distress
That men call joy, the littleness
That men call life – as birds are free.
So in the dewy morning hour
She hanged herself within the tower,

Beside her portrait, spirit-fair,
With these words written: 'We come again,
And ours the house of Colomen.'

Her cousins came and found her there,
While high against the painted dawn
Her pigeons - rosy, white and fawn,
Coal-black and mottled - wheeled in the air.
But while they gazed, weeping aloud,
Around the tower a silence fell.
The doves wheeled high: they could not tell
Which were birds and which was cloud.

A haunted silence held the tower,
Wherein the portrait's living eyes
Watched the dead lady with surprise,
Like a flower that gazes on a flower.

No doves returned there evermore.
The spiders wove about the door
Intricate tapestries of time,
That held the dew and held the rime.
And from the house of Colomen,
Like water from a frozen strand,
Failed the voices of maids and men,
Shrivelled the heart, shrivelled the hand,
Till there within the arching wood
No face was left but the painted face,
No sound was left of the human race,
But only the sound of doves that cooed
Sadly, intermittently -
Wheeling doves that none can see

But dying men who wander here
And see a picture, glassy-clear,
Where the milky hawthorn-blossom falls
And from the elm a blackbird calls:
Then softly from the ruined cote
A pigeon coos - and faint, remote,
A hundred pigeons answer low,
Voicing the lady's ancient woe;
And then they see her, very fair
And fragile in the scented air;
On arms and shoulders doves alight,
Multiple-tinted, like a bright
Tapestry that time has faded.
Softly purple, lilac-shaded,
The lady standeth, like a tree
Bent down with blossom. ...

TO THE WORLD

You took the rare blue from my cloudy sky;
You shot the one bird in my silent wood;
You crushed my rose - one rose alone had I.
You have not known. You have not understood.

I would have shown you pictures I have seen
Of unimagined mountains, plains and seas;
I would have made you songs of leafy green,
If you had left me some small ecstasies.

Now let the one dear field be only field,
That was a garden for the mighty gods.
Take you its corn. I keep its better yield -
The glory that I found within its clods.

LAST POEMS

MAGIC

Out of their shallow pools
The grouse whirr, jeering at us fools
That have not known how all things grow estranged
Except old Magic, who with gipsy fingers
Forever sews, unwearied and unchanged,
The splendid purple garments of the hills.
They sleep within the silence that she fills
With lullabies, singing beneath her breath
Of things so long before and so long after death
That he who listens fears her, yet he lingers.

SWALLOWS

The swallows pass in restless companies.
Against the pink-flowered may, one shining breast
Throbs momentary music – then, possessed
With motion, sweeps on some new enterprise.
Unquiet in heart, I hear their eager cries
And see them dart to their nests beneath the eaves;
Within my spirit is a voice that grieves,
Reminding me of empty autumn skies.
Nor can we rest in Nature's dear delight:
June droops to winter, and the sun droops west.
Flight is our life. We build our crumbling nest
Beneath the dark eaves of the infinite,
We sing our song in beauty's fading tree,
And flash forth, migrant, into mystery.

DUST

On burning ploughlands, faintly blue with wheat,
A three-horse roller toils, the wandering dust
A nimbus round it. Shadow-coloured hills
Huddle beyond - hump-shouldered, kingly-headed
Or eel-shaped; sinister, tortured - waiting still,
Beneath the purposeful, secretive sky,
The multitudinous years
That soon or late will melt them.
So I have felt them
In all their static beauty only fit for tears,
Like those that toil along the blood-red weald
With their own death-dust round them for sole glory
Under the falcon wings
Of dawn, the red night's carrion-swoop,
The intolerable emptiness of air.

Long, long ago I thought on all these things:
Long, long ago I loved them.

ROSE-BERRIES

The green pine-needles shiver glassily,
Each cased in ice. Harsh winter, grey and dun,
Shuts out the sun.
But with live, scarlet fire,
Enfolding seed of sweet Junes yet to be,
Rose-berries melt the snow, and burn above
The thorny briar,
Like beauty with its deathless seed of love.

ON THE WILD HILL

Would God I were there, on the wild hill
Where the ponies with wet fetlocks wade in morasses
Starred with yellow mimulus, drinking the chill
Brown water! Where the bright foals, black and bay,
Run to their dams through the dark blue day,
As the shadow of a hawk passes.

If I might be there in the grave dawn,
Stumbling on a curlew's nest beneath its spread
Of flowering heather, and seeing across the lawn,
Sheep-mown, the creamy, pencilled curlew chickens run,
Quick and bright as water in the sun,
Hiding in a fresh green bracken-bed!

If only I might watch the old curlews drifting
Down the silver summer air like tawny leaves!
Hear their icy, elfin voices uplifting
The warm rich veils of silence and content,
Discovering some chill presentiment,
Like a fugitive soul that grieves.

THE LAND WITHIN

This is a land of forests, and of meres
Stirless and deep, replenished with my tears.
Here the pine harps, and many voices moan
Within the cedar, crying, 'Lone! Alone!'
Sharp on green heaven the green ice peaks arise
Through the deep snows of thawless purities.
Ten thousand stars are drowned within the lake,
Beneath grey ice. And while the branches break,
The million crystals shining there arow
Can never fall, though every tempest blow.
Only the rush, with brown and broken spear,
Tells of the host of summer mustering here,
Where now the reeds, encrusted stiff with glass,
Sound a faint music, faintly sigh 'Alas!'
Where are the birds that with blue flash would make
Traffic between blue sky and bluer lake,
Ripping the water with a long, keen wing,
Then setting rosy breasts arow to sing?
O, they are fled, my soul! Fled far away
To some gold tree in Spain or Africa.

Was there a sound of leaves here once, and streams
Gurgling on pebbles? (In dreams, my soul! in dreams).
Galleons of golden lilies then could ride
Safely, though coot and moorhen stirred the tide,
Swimming with all their young; and loud sweet cries
Fell from the mountains where the curlew haunted
Green mossy cwms, sun-drenched and thrice enchanted;

And somewhere in the lake's confused reflections,
Remote and fair as childhood's recollections,
Smothered in wavering lilac leaves, and blurred
With bloom, the shadow of a gable stirred
With every tide, and a twisted chimney flowered
In pale blue smoke, that in the water towered
Downward. And through those deeps, pillared and aisled,
Came a brown woodman, and a boy who smiled,
Running towards the shifting wicket-gate,
And waved an under-water hand, to spy
One leaning from the casement - that was I.

Where was that cottage with its lilac trees,
Its windows wide, its garden drowsed with bees?
Where stood the echoing glade whence the faggot came
To turn the evening hours to one warm flame?
And that brown woodman, where and whence was he -
That woodman, with the eyes that dazzled me
Far more than rosy fire or golden gleams
Of April? O, in dreams, my soul! in dreams.

ON RECEIVING A BOX OF SPRING FLOWERS IN LONDON

So the old, dear freemasonry goes on –
    The busy life, the laughter-under-sod,
The leafy hosts with spear and gonfalon
    Guarding the earthy mysteries of God.

I did not think the violets came so soon,
    Yet here are five, and all my room is sweet;
And here's an aconite – a golden moon
    Shining where all her raying leaflets meet;

And here a snowdrop, finely veined – ah, see!
    Fresh from the artist's hand, and folded close:
She only waits the sunshine and the bee;
    Then she will open like a golden rose.

TO A BLACKBIRD SINGING IN LONDON

Sing on, dear bird! Bring the old rapturous pain,
In this great town, where I no welcome find.
Show me the murmuring forest in your mind,
And April's fragile cups, brimful of rain.
O sing me far away, that I may hear
The voice of grass, and, weeping, may be blind
To slights and lies and friends that prove unkind,
Sing till my soul dissolves into a tear,
Glimmering within a chaliced daffodil.
So, when the stately sun with burning breath
Absorbs my being, I'll dream that he is Death,
Great Death, the undisdainful. By his will
No more unlovely, haunting all things fair,
I'll seek some kinder life in the golden air.

GOODBYE TO MORNING

I will say goodbye to morning, with her eyes
Of gold, her shell-pale robe and crocus-crown.
Once her green veils enmeshed me, following down
The dewy hills of heaven: with young surprise
The daisies eyed me, and the pointed leaves
Came swiftly in green fire to meet the sun:
The elves from every hollow, one by one,
Laughed shrilly. But the wind of evening grieves
In the changing wood. Like people sad and old,
The white-lashed daisies sleep, and on my sight
Looms my new sombre comrade, ancient night.
His eyes dream dark on death; all stark and cold
His fingers, and on his wild forehead gleams
My morning wreath of withered and frozen dreams.

'THE BIRDS WILL SING'

The birds will sing when I am gone
To stranger-folk with stranger-ways.
Without a break they'll whistle on
In close and flowery orchard deeps,
Where once I loved them, nights and days,
And never reck of one that weeps.

The bud that slept within the bark
When I was there, will break her bars –
And round into a world, and spread
Beneath the silver dews and stars,
Nor miss my bent, attentive head.

SAFE

Under a blossoming tree
Let me lie down,
With one blackbird to sing to me
In the evenings brown.
Safe from the world's long importunity –
The endless talk, the critical, sly stare,
The trifling social days – and unaware
Of all the bitter thoughts they have of me,
Low in the grass, deep in the daisies,
I shall sleep sound, safe from their blames and praises.

FAREWELL TO BEAUTY

'Their being is to be perceived.' Berkeley

Let fall your golden showers, laburnum tree!
Break the grey casket of your buds for me -
Soon I shall go where never gold is seen,
And who will be with you as I have been?

Quick with your silver notes, O silver bird!
Wistful, I listen for the song I heard
Many a day, but soon shall hear no more,
For summoning winds are out along the shore.

All things so early fade - swiftly pass over,
As autumn bees desert the withering clover.
Now, with the bee, I sing immortal June;
How soon both song and bee are gone - how soon!

Who'll watch the clover secretly unclose?
Finger the sycamore buds, afire with rose?
Trace the mauve veins of the anemone?
Know the peculiar scent of every tree?

Maybe the solemn hill, the enchanted plain
Will be but arable and wild again,
Losing the purple bloom they wore for me -
The dreaming god I could so clearly see.

NOTES

THE HERITAGE. Written in 1907 when M.W. (then Mary Meredith) was ill with a recurrence of Graves' Disease and though confined to bed for many weeks continued to write, propped up by pillows.

THE LOST ORCHARD. Belonging to the same period of illness, this poem refers to the meadows, stream and orchard which M.W. could see from her bedroom window at Maesbrook, the old Mill House in Meole Brace village. The MS of the poem bears the name Meole Brace. First published in the Sunday Pictorial , 25 April, 1920.

THE WATER OUSEL. Written during the early days at Maesbrook when M.W. spent many hours watching birds and the minutiae of nature along the stream in the grounds and the banks of the little River Rea. Her father constructed the waterfalls. First published in The Nation and the Athenaeum, Vol. 29, 30 July, 1921, p. 648.

FOXGLOVES. The foxglove is a wild flower characteristic of Shropshire and with many associations in country lore known to M.W. (see Gone to Earth and Precious Bane).

FAIRY-LED. Reminiscent of Christina Rossetti's 'Goblin Market' : M.W. was influenced by both of the Rossettis (one of her poems, not included here, was written in tribute to Christina Rossetti). Lay-out here as in MS

CATERINA TO CAMOENS. Luis Vaz de Camoes (Eng. Camoens), 1524-1580, the great Portuguese poet (lyric, epic, dramatic). Catarina de Ataide is thought by some critics to have inspired many of Camoens' poems, but as he himself said in a sonnet 'em varias flamas variamente ardia' ('I burnt myself at many flames').

THE VAGRANT. At this stage of her development, M.W. had already broken away from the conventional religion of her upbringing though she continued to attend Church of England services as she did not wish to upset her father, a keen churchman. The poem defines her spiritual yearning, a pantheistic mysticism still coloured with Christian elements, the impulse behind much of her writing at this time. First published in The English Review, Vol. 19, January 1915, pp. 134-35.

THE LITTLE SORROW. The poem refers to her father's ageing and his death. The middle stanza was excluded when the poem was published in PSJ (Poems and The Spring of Joy), but I included the full version, as in the MS, in MWCPP (Mary Webb : Collected Prose and Poems).

UNFINISHED EMBROIDERY. Strongly autobiographical; MS dated 5 January.

TREASURES. This might seem a sentimental, idealised picture of G.E.M., but Kenneth Meredith (M.W.'s brother) has stressed that it is a most accurate depiction of the qualities and personality of their father. See also M.W.'s portrait of her father as John Arden in The Golden Arrow (her first novel).

JOY. M.W. expresses here her understanding of the significance of suffering and her own experience of progress through a dark night of the soul. Reminiscent of the stanzas of the mystic, St. John of the Cross.

THE GOBLET. See The Golden Arrow : 'in her soul the crystal of her pride shivered into fragments' (of Deborah's love for Stephen). Descriptions in the novels sometimes have counterparts in the poems.

TODAY and ISOLDE. Written at Weston-super-Mare where the newly married Webbs were living 1912-14 (at Penrose, Landemann Circus, not far from the headland).Henry taught at a Boys'Boarding School in the Circus - M.W. did not like unexpected visitors or, in fact, any intrusions on their privacy. These poems reflect her insecurity.

HUMBLE FOLK. The lane referred to is that which passes by Rose Cottage, Pontesbury. The Webbs returned to Shropshire in 1914 and were living as full-time writers at Rose Cottage (M.W. wrote The Golden Arrow there). This poem,and those which follow in the Pontesbury series, were written in the happiest period of her married life.

THE LITTLE HILL. The hill described here is Pontesford Hill, not far from Rose Cottage, one of their favourite walking places up through the larches.

MARKET DAY. Reflects M.W.'s exhilaration in her market venture. She worked the large kitchen garden at Rose Cottage and sold the produce at Shrewsbury market as part of her war effort ('Dig For Victory'). She often walked the nine miles to market and nine miles back again, making only a little money as she sold her produce very cheaply. Her fascination with markets is seen in the vivid descriptions in her novels (GA, SFS, PB).

AN OLD WOMAN. M.W.'s compassion is evident here. She visited old women in the Workhouse (some were guests at her wedding), and called on old cottagers. The old woman of this poem was undoubtedly known personally by her. See also

the short story 'Blessed Are The Meek' in <u>Armour Wherein He Trusted</u>. This
poem was first published in <u>The English Review</u>, Vol.21, October 1915, p. 236.
THE LAD OUT THERE. M.W.'s three brothers were serving at the Western Front.
She was a devoted sister, worried incessantly about their safety, and sent
each of them a copy of this poem. Kenneth received his copy and a letter
on his arrival in France with the Canadian Ambulance Unit.
AN ESTRAY. Written at Chester in the summer of 1916, when M.W. was living
with her mother and sister, Olive ; H.B.L.W. was teaching at the King's
School. M.W. became severely depressed due to the war (it was at the time
of the Somme catastrophe), the military atmosphere of Chester, tensions
between herself and her mother, acute homesickness for Shropshire. The
third stanza was omitted when the poem was published in <u>Fifty-One Poems</u>
(prepared by H.B.L.W. for publication); the MS shows no deletion. The poem
appears here as in M.W.'s typescript (full version first published in
MWCPP). Estrays – hill ponies and cattle gone astray from pasture.
THE MESSENGER. A later version of 'The Thought'.
PRESENCES. The scene here is Lyth Hill with its Little Wood (where M.W.
was living at Spring Cottage).
VIROCONIUM. The Roman City at Wroxeter, near Leighton where M.W. was born.
She returned many times, fascinated, as Wilfred Owen was, by the ruins.
'The pillars stand, with alien grace,/In churches of a younger race' :
for instance, the nearby church at Wroxeter. Excavations of Viroconium
were abandoned in 1914, resumed in 1923 when M.W. wrote the essay 'The
Return of the Romans : A Dream of Uriconium' (MWCPP). The poem was first
published in <u>The English Review</u>, 1924.
GREEN RAIN. The opening lines are thought by some critics to be a
verbal echo of Housman's 'About the woodlands I will go/ And see the
cherry hung with snow'. In considering this, it should be kept in mind
that M.W. and Housman were steeped in many of the same sources, such
as the Bible, Coverdale's translation of the Psalms, ballads and folk
verse. Both M.W. and Housman make use of traditional four foot iambic
lines and octosyllabic couplets which were the basis of much folk
verse. In this case, both poets drew on a local folk song ; and in this
area of countryside, the metaphor of snow for blossom is common. M.W.

is in fact describing the Little Wood on Lyth Hill where she spent hours of each day. The poem was first published in <u>The Spectator</u>, 24 March 1923, p.512, and subsequently in <u>Living Age</u>, Vol. 317, 26 May 1923, p.488.

THE WOOD. Again the scene is the Little Wood on Lyth Hill.

MY OWN TOWN. At one of its levels of meaning, the poem is describing Shrewsbury.

THE NEIGHBOUR'S CHILDREN. M.W. was approx. forty, and childless, when she wrote this poem. Her generosity to children (especially the destitute ones of Shrewsbury) became legendary. At Lyth Hill she was called 'Ladysmock' by the children; every Christmas she gave each child a gift. Mrs. Thorne was her neighbour and it is her children who are those of the poem.

ANNE'S BOOK. First published in <u>The Nation and The Athenaeum</u>, Vol.29 no.15, 9 July 1921, p.541; and in <u>Living Age</u>, Vol.311, I October 1921,p.58.

TO G.D.M. Written for her brother, George Douglas Meredith. The MS is dated 15 September 1919.

THE WATCHER. First published in <u>The Spectator</u>, 3 December 1921,p. 743.

ABSENCE. Written at Lyth Hill; the MS is dated June 1921. M.W. was alone at Spring Cottage, H.B.L.W. in London (see <u>The Flower of Light</u>, p. 226).

COLOMEN. One of M.W.'s last pieces, most probably not revised. Written at Lyth Hill when she was slowly dying. In this poem she is allegorising the breakdown of her relationship with her beloved H.B.L.W. who, estranged from her, was involved with a former pupil (he married this girl after M.W.'s death). Her own death-wish is implied here. The name 'Colomen' was suggested to her by 'Columbine' (according to H.B.L.W. who found the poem among her papers after her death); there was a dovecote nearby and also the wood-pigeons in the Little Wood which, as she sat or stood very still, used to settle on her arms and shoulders.

DUST. The hills described here are the Strettons, the Long Mynd, the Stiperstones, all of which are seen from Lyth Hill.

ON THE WILD HILL. The MS is dated 1922. The Webbs were then living at Leinster Square, Bayswater.

ON RECEIVING A BOX OF SPRING FLOWERS IN LONDON. The flowers were sent by Mrs. Thorne from M.W.'s own garden at Spring Cottage.

TO A BLACKBIRD SINGING IN LONDON. That M.W. was desperately unhappy, ill and disillusioned is evident in this and the following autobiographical poems. The blackbird sang in the lime tree of her tiny Hampstead garden.